The
SUMMER
SOLSTICE

*"The sun is a fiery stone,
a little larger than Greece."*
Anaxagoras, 434 B.C.

To Rose Soglin
E.J.

Library of Congress Cataloging-in-Publication Data
Jackson, Ellen B., 1943–
The summer solstice / Ellen Jackson;
illustrated by Jan Davey Ellis.
p. cm.
Includes bibliographical references.
ISBN 0-7613-1623-X (lib. bdg.) ISBN 0-7613-1283-8 (tr.)
1. Summer solstice—Juvenile literature. [1. Summer solstice.
2. Festivals.] I. Ellis, Jan Davey, ill. II. Title.
GT4995.S85   J33   2001
394.263—dc21 00-041870

Published by The Millbrook Press, Inc.
2 Old New Milford Road
Brookfield, Connecticut 06804
www.millbrookpress.com

The
SUMMER SOLSTICE

Ellen Jackson   *Illustrated by* **Jan Davey Ellis**

THE MILLBROOK PRESS   BROOKFIELD, CONNECTICUT

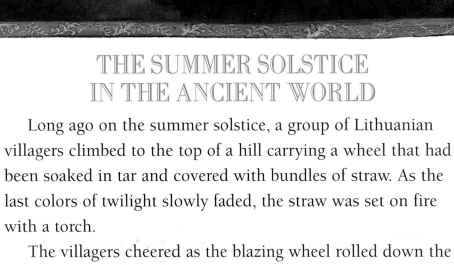

THE SUMMER SOLSTICE
IN THE ANCIENT WORLD

Long ago on the summer solstice, a group of Lithuanian villagers climbed to the top of a hill carrying a wheel that had been soaked in tar and covered with bundles of straw. As the last colors of twilight slowly faded, the straw was set on fire with a torch.

The villagers cheered as the blazing wheel rolled down the hill and into the river. Some of them jumped back and forth over the flames. The wheel was still burning as it sank into the water, and the villagers considered that a good omen. The harvest would be plentiful—even though the sun, like the wheel, would soon begin its descent in the sky.

People have always looked up at the sun with wonder and gratitude. From earliest times, the sun has been recognized as the source of warmth and light. Without the sun, the world would be cold and dark, and life could not exist. The sun was so important to ancient people, it was sometimes viewed as a god. People wanted to celebrate the day when the sun was at its highest point in the sky—the summer solstice.

In North and South America and in Europe, people built structures to help them track the movements of the life-giving sun. More than two thousand years ago, Native American tribes in the United States and Canada built circles of stone. These circles usually had one spoke that pointed to the place where the sun rose on the summer solstice.

The Chumash Indians of California cut holes in the walls or ceilings of caves. Through the holes a beam of light shone on sacred art painted on the walls of the cave—but only on the summer solstice. The Anasazi Indians of New Mexico painted two spirals on a rock in Chaco Canyon. At noon on the summer solstice, a dagger of light pointed to the center of one of the spirals.

The summer solstice was the most important day of the year in ancient Egypt. Not only was the sun at its peak, but the waters of the Nile river would begin to rise at this time, too. The Egyptians held a special festival at the summer solstice to honor the goddess Isis. They believed that Isis was mourning for her dead husband, Osiris, and that the tears from her eyes made the Nile swell and overflow.

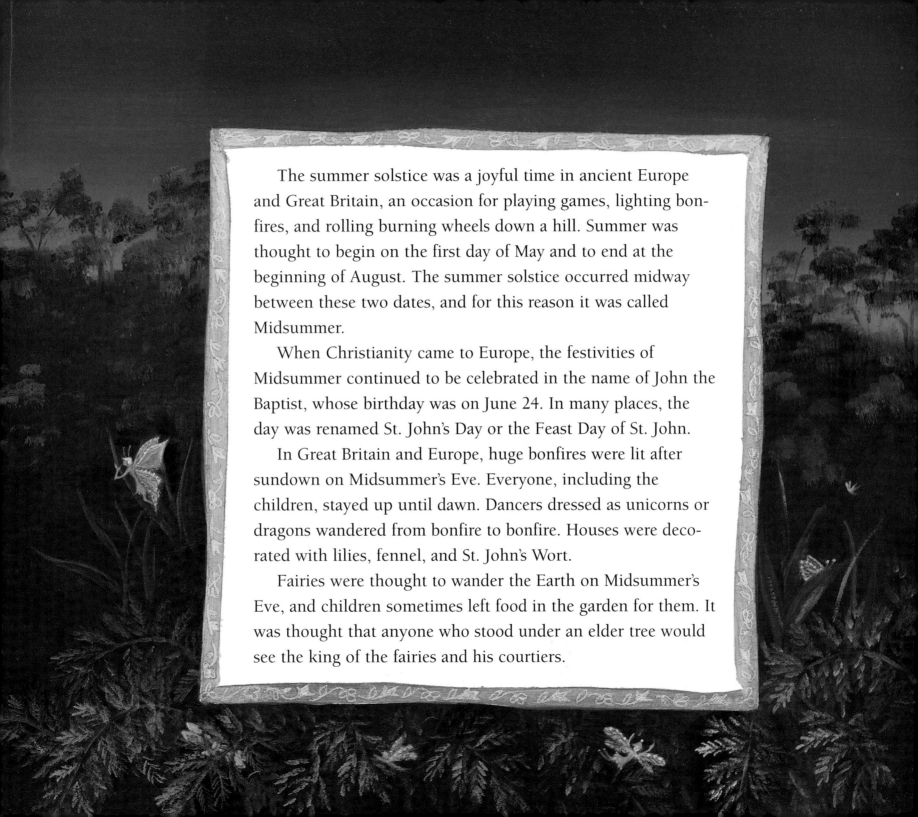

The summer solstice was a joyful time in ancient Europe and Great Britain, an occasion for playing games, lighting bonfires, and rolling burning wheels down a hill. Summer was thought to begin on the first day of May and to end at the beginning of August. The summer solstice occurred midway between these two dates, and for this reason it was called Midsummer.

When Christianity came to Europe, the festivities of Midsummer continued to be celebrated in the name of John the Baptist, whose birthday was on June 24. In many places, the day was renamed St. John's Day or the Feast Day of St. John.

In Great Britain and Europe, huge bonfires were lit after sundown on Midsummer's Eve. Everyone, including the children, stayed up until dawn. Dancers dressed as unicorns or dragons wandered from bonfire to bonfire. Houses were decorated with lilies, fennel, and St. John's Wort.

Fairies were thought to wander the Earth on Midsummer's Eve, and children sometimes left food in the garden for them. It was thought that anyone who stood under an elder tree would see the king of the fairies and his courtiers.

Legends told of the marvelous events that were said to occur on Midsummer's Eve in the British Isles. Cadbury Castle in Somerset, England, was built on a hill that was said to be hollow. According to legend, every seven years at Midsummer, the hillside opened up and King Arthur and his knights rode forth to water their horses. Once the horses had quenched their thirst, the King and his men rode back into the hill to sleep for another seven years.

The Shetland Islanders told stories of strange, bewitched creatures called selkies. For most of the year, selkies were said to live in the ocean as seals. But on Midsummer's Eve, the selkies would come ashore, shed their skins, and dance all night. At dawn they returned to the ocean to live as seals for another year.

In Ireland, people would sometimes walk around the solstice bonfires reciting prayers. After the prayers, the fun would begin. Music, dancing, and storytelling were part of the festivities. When the fires had gone out, farmers would sprinkle the ashes on their fields to bless the crops.

In a region called Bohemia, which is now part of the Czech Republic, girls made wreaths to prepare for the summer solstice. When the bonfires were lit, the girls would stand on one side of the fire, while the boys stood on the other side. Each girl would throw a wreath across the fire to her sweetheart. The singed wreaths were thought to prevent sickness, and they were kept for good luck.

In many countries in Europe, people believed that herbs had special powers if they were gathered on the summer solstice. Hazel branches cut on the eve of the solstice were used to search for water or gold and precious jewels. St. John's Wort, which bloomed at the end of June, was supposed to frighten away evil spirits. Other herbs, such as chamomile and thyme, were thrown into the bonfires to add their aromas to the smoke.

Fruit, grains, and berries begin to ripen in early summer. The people of Swaziland, a country in southeastern Africa, held a first fruits ceremony to renew the strength of the king and the Swazi nation at the solstice. During the ceremony, the king ate the fruits of the new season. Then he joined his warriors in a special dance. The ceremony was intended to drive away the evil of the past year and prepare everyone for the year to come.

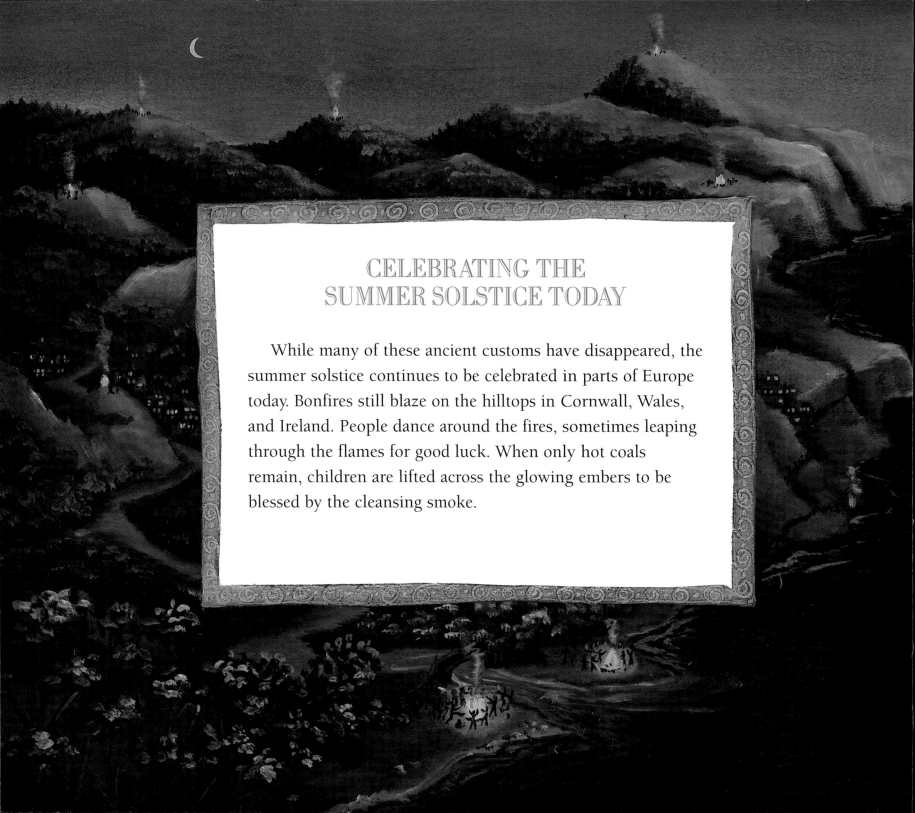

CELEBRATING THE
SUMMER SOLSTICE TODAY

While many of these ancient customs have disappeared, the summer solstice continues to be celebrated in parts of Europe today. Bonfires still blaze on the hilltops in Cornwall, Wales, and Ireland. People dance around the fires, sometimes leaping through the flames for good luck. When only hot coals remain, children are lifted across the glowing embers to be blessed by the cleansing smoke.

In Scandinavia, summer is very brief, and most people want to be outdoors during the warmest part of the year. In parts of Norway, the sun doesn't set at all from mid-May to July. On Midsummer's Eve, the Norwegians light fires in the mountains, in the valleys, and along the shores. Musicians play, and people in folk costumes dance all night long.

In Sweden, homes, apartments, buildings, and even cars are decked with birch boughs and flowers. A pole, called a *majstang,* is decorated with leaves, streamers, and flowers, and the Swedish flag is placed at the very top. The villagers flock to the village green, where they laugh and cheer as the pole is raised and wedged into a deep hole. Children join hands and circle around the pole, while the adults, dressed in traditional costumes, dance the Windmill Dance or the Three Karls Polka.

Communities in the United States and Canada also observe the solstice. In Santa Barbara, California, people celebrate with a noontime parade featuring fantastic costumes, music, dancing, and street theater. In Anchorage, Alaska, the Goldpanners baseball team, which has produced several major league players, plays a nighttime game using no artificial lights. In Quebec, Canada, St. John's Day is celebrated with games, races, bonfires, and parades.

While everyone enjoys the balmy days of summer, people today seldom worry about the dark days ahead. Scientists now know why the days are longer in the summer and shorter in the winter. The seasons are caused by the changing position of Earth in relation to the sun.

If you stick one toothpick in the top of an orange, and another toothpick in the bottom, you can see how the position of Earth creates the seasons. In a dark room, shine a flashlight (which represents the sun) directly at the middle or center part of the orange (which represents Earth). Tilt the North Pole toothpick slightly toward the light. You will see that most of the light shines on the top part of the orange.

This is the position of the sun and Earth during the Northern Hemisphere's summer. Now tilt the North Pole slightly away from the light. This is the position of Earth at the time of the Northern Hemisphere's winter solstice, when it receives less sunlight than the Southern Hemisphere. People living in the tropics, near the equator, do not have true seasons. There, the amount of light is always the same, and the temperature is always warm.

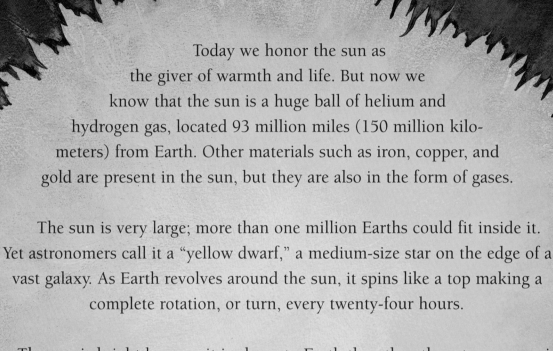

Today we honor the sun as
the giver of warmth and life. But now we
know that the sun is a huge ball of helium and
hydrogen gas, located 93 million miles (150 million kilo-
meters) from Earth. Other materials such as iron, copper, and
gold are present in the sun, but they are also in the form of gases.

The sun is very large; more than one million Earths could fit inside it.
Yet astronomers call it a "yellow dwarf," a medium-size star on the edge of a
vast galaxy. As Earth revolves around the sun, it spins like a top making a
complete rotation, or turn, every twenty-four hours.

The sun is bright because it is closer to Earth than the other stars we see in
the sky. It is only one of countless trillions of stars, but it is special to us. It is
the source of almost every form of energy on Earth. All living things rely on
the amazing sun for their existence.

The summer solstice is a time of joy, a time to dance and be
happy. At the solstice new leaves grow on trees, and the air is
fragrant and filled with the music of birdsong. The golden
sun blazes high in the sky. On this day at least, it
seems as if summer will last forever.

A SUMMER SOLSTICE STORY
How Summer Came to the Island People

The following story was adapted from an ancient Hawaiian chant that tells of the adventures of Maui, a mythological hero of Polynesia.

Once a boy named Maui lived with his mother on a beautiful green island in the Pacific Ocean. Maui's mother, Hina, worked all day making tapa cloth from wet bark. Each day Hina pounded the wet cloth on a long wooden board, while Maui cast his nets into the ocean.

But the days were too short. There was never enough time for the tapa to dry. The sun seemed to race across the sky, and the work was never finished.

"That sun is in such a hurry," said Hina. "Almost as soon as we get up, it's time to go to bed. Even the plants are withering."

Maui looked around. It was true. He realized that if something was to be done, he'd have to do it. So just before dawn, Maui set his noose traps not far from the volcano Halea-kala, where the sun sleeps at night. Then he waited.

Finally the rooster crowed. Maui looked up to see the first ray of sun creeping down the side of the volcano. The ray alighted on a rock. It lingered on a bush. Then it stepped into the first noose. Whap! The noose tightened and held it fast.

A second ray followed the first. It groped around looking for the first ray. Before long, it too was trapped. Then came another ray, and another. Soon all sixteen rays of the sun were caught in the sixteen nooses.

The scowling face of the sun appeared over the rim of Halea-kala. When it saw what had happened, the sun raged and spit fire. Sparks and flames lit up the sky. Maui jumped up and tied all the ropes to a nearby tree.

"Let me go!" screamed the sun, thrashing and yanking at the ropes. A blast of heat hit the boy in the face and singed his hair.

"Stop that!" said Maui. "Or I'll cut you down to size."

The sun looked at Maui's ax. It sighed. Then it grew dimmer.

"What do you want?" asked the sun in a sulky voice.

"I want you to slow down," said Maui. "You are going too fast. The plants are withering and the tapa cloth won't dry. From now on, you must take your time, so the days are long and filled with light."

"I will go more slowly, but only some of the time," said the sun. "In the summer, I will go slow. In the winter, I will go as fast as I please. That's fair, isn't it?"

"That's good enough," said Maui. He was tired of fighting.

Then Maui cut the ropes and the sun rose into the sky, taking the strands of rope with him. Maui looked down. The ropes floated in the sky like clouds, making wispy shadows in the sand.

"When the people see the cloud ropes," said the sun, "they will remember my bargain with you. For these are the ropes that bind Earth and Heaven together."

And Maui and his people lived in harmony with the sun forever after.

**Author's Note: Portions of the original story of Maui were omitted for brevity. This story was adapted from *How Maui Slowed the Sun* by Suelyn Ching Tune and *Maui-Full-of-Tricks: A Legend of Old Hawaii* by Vivian L. Thompson.

Midsummer Activities

SIDEWALK SUNDIAL

As Earth rotates, the sun appears to move across the sky. But it is actually Earth that is moving. If something blocks the light of the sun, a shadow is created. Here is an experiment with shadows to help you observe Earth's rotation or movement.

You will need:

1 paper cup
Large sheet of plain white paper
Marking pens—red, green, and blue

1. Begin this experiment about ten o'clock in the morning on a sunny day. Find a place that will remain in the sun for several hours.
2. Place the piece of paper in the sunlight. Put the paper cup on top of the paper. Put a rock in the cup to hold it in place.
3. Trace the shadow of the cup with the red pen. At the bottom of the paper put a red dot and then write the time next to the dot.
4. Repeat this experiment in one-half hour, using the green pen. Repeat in an hour with the blue pen.

What has happened to the shadow? Why? Repeat the experiment at different seasons.

COOKING WITH THE SUN

Here is a recipe that uses the sun's energy to create a tasty treat.

You will need:

1 package of graham crackers
1 package of small marshmallows
4 or 5 plain milk chocolate candy bars
Large glass baking pan with glass lid

1. Choose a place in the direct sunlight away from pets or other animals. This experiment must be done on a very warm day.
2. Line the bottom of the baking pan with graham crackers. On each cracker place a square of chocolate topped with marshmallows.
3. Cover the baking pan with the lid and place it in the sunshine.
4. Let it sit in the sunshine until the chocolate and marshmallows melt. Top each cracker with another, sandwich style, to make the treat.

SUN SNACKS

The sun is extremely hot. The sun's surface, which is called the photosphere, is approximately 10,000 degrees F (5,500 degrees C). The sun's atmosphere, called the corona, is hotter than the surface. It is approximately 3,600,000 degrees F (2 million degrees C). The very center of the sun, called the core, is the hottest part of the sun. Temperatures in the core reach 27 million degrees F (about 15 million degrees C).

Here is a recipe/puzzle to help you remember these facts about the sun.

You will need:

Several sliced bananas
Canned pineapple rings
Candy corn
Plate

Using one slice of banana, one pineapple ring, and a handful of candy corn, put the pieces together on a plate to make a picture of the sun.

Can you guess which ingredient will be the core of the sun? The photosphere? The corona? Can you remember which part of the sun is the hottest? The coolest?

Eat and enjoy!

BOHEMIAN WREATH

The girls of Bohemia made flower wreaths to celebrate the solstice. Here is a wreath that you can make.

You will need:
A bundle of tall grass or reeds
String
Scissors
Bright-colored ribbon
Summer flowers
Small plant clippers

1. Pick summer weeds, herbs, and flowers, and clip their stems to 4 or 5 inches (10 or 13 cm) in length. Hang the flowers together in a bunch, stems side up, in a dark, dry place for several weeks.
2. Also gather enough long stems of grass or reeds to make a bundle a few inches (about 8 cm) across. Allow the grass or reeds to dry for a week.
3. Soak the bundle of grass or reeds in the bathtub for about an hour. Drain.
4. Tie the reeds or grass together in a circle with the string. Twist a piece of ribbon around the wreath in a candy cane or barber pole pattern. Loop the end of the ribbon around itself and tie.
5. Weave the dried flowers and plants into the wreath by tucking them into the ribbon. Trim extra plant material if necessary. Hang the wreath on a door or wall.

SOLSTICE TREE

In Switzerland, fir trees were sometimes decorated with leaves, flowers, and ribbons at the summer solstice. Choose a special tree and decorate it to say thank you for the shade, nuts, and fruit that trees provide.

You will need:

Popped popcorn
Raisins
Pinecones
Flowers
Leaves
Dental floss
Needle with a large eye
Scissors

1. Thread the needle with dental floss, and string the popcorn and raisins together to make decorations for the tree.
2. String flowers and leaves together to make garlands.
3. Tie individual flowers and pinecones to the tree's branches.

You can also make ornaments or garlands out of gummy candy.

WORD PLAY

There are many English words that contain the word "sun." How many can you name?

You will need:

Paper
Pencil
Dictionary

1. Without looking in the dictionary, make a list of English words that contain the word "sun."
2. Consult the dictionary to find other "sun" words you may have forgotten.
3. On the back of the paper write "It Happened on Sunday."
4. Choose three "sun" words from your list. Make up a story using your three words.

BIBLIOGRAPHY

Berg, Elizabeth. *(Egypt) Festivals of the World*, Milwaukee, Wisconsin: Gareth Stevens, 1997.

Epstein, Sam, and Beryl Epstein. *A Holiday Book: European Folk Festivals*, Champaign, Illinois: Garrard, 1968.

Heinberg, Richard. *Celebrate the Solstice: Honoring the Earth's Seasonal Rhythms Through Festival and Ceremony*, Wheaton, Illinois: Theosophical Publishing House, 1993.

Helfman, Elizabeth S. *Celebrating Nature, Rites and Ceremonies Around the World*, New York: Seabury, 1969.

Henderson, Helene, and Sue Ellen Thompson, Eds. *Holidays, Festivals, and Celebrations of the World Dictionary*, Detroit, Michigan: Omnigraphics, 1994.

Henes, Donna. *Seasons, Cycles, & Celebrations*, New York: Berkeley, 1996.

Markle, Sandra. *Exploring Summer*, New York: Atheneum, 1987.

Nickerson, Betty. *Celebrate the Sun*, New York: J.B. Lippincott, 1969.

Olcott, William Tyler. *Sun Lore of All Ages: A Collection of Myths and Legends Concerning the Sun and Its Worship*, New York: G.P. Putnam's Sons, 1914.

Rosen, Mike. *Summer Festivals*, New York: Bookwright, 1991.

Spicer, Dorothy Gladys. *Festivals of Western Europe*, New York: H.W. Wilson, 1958.

Thompson, Vivian L. *Maui-Full-of-Tricks: A Legend of Old Hawaii*, San Carlos, California: Golden Gate Junior Books, 1970.

Tune, Suelyn Ching. *How Maui Slowed the Sun*, Honolulu: University of Hawaii Press, 1988.